one watermelon seed

story by Celia Barker Lottridge • pictures by Karen Patkau

toronto
oxford university press

CANADIAN CATALOGUING IN PUBLICATION DATA
Lottridge, Celia
One watermelon seed
ISBN 0-19-540735-0
1. Counting — Juvenile literature. I. Patkau
Karen. II. Title.
QA113.L67 1985   j513'2   C85-098791-1

OXFORD is a trademark of Oxford University Press
Text © Celia Barker Lottridge 1986
Illustrations © Karen Patkau 1986
3 4 5 6 7 — 97 96 95 94 93
Printed and bound in Hong Kong

Max and Josephine planted a garden.

1 They planted one watermelon seed … and it grew.

They planted two pumpkin seeds ... and they grew. **2**

3 Max planted three eggplants . . . and they grew.

Josephine planted four pepper seeds ... and they grew. **4**

5 Then she planted five tomato plants ... and they grew.

Max planted six blueberry bushes … and they grew. **6**

7   And seven strawberry plants … and they grew.

Josephine planted eight bean seeds ... and they grew. **8**

9 And nine seed potatoes ... and they grew.

They planted ten corn seeds ... and they grew. 10

The rain fell and the sun shone. The seeds and the leaves, the stalks and the vines grew and grew and grew.

Max and Josephine weeded and watered and waited. One day they looked at their garden and saw there was plenty to pick. So ...

10 They picked ten watermelons, big and green.

And twenty pumpkins, glowing orange. **20**

30 Max picked thirty eggplants, dark and purple,

and forty peppers, shiny yellow. **40**

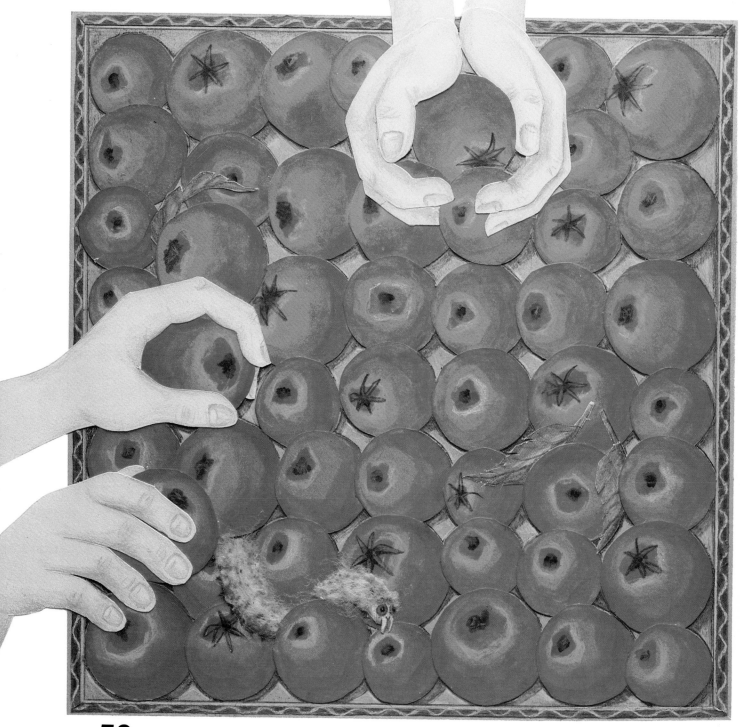

50 They both picked fifty tomatoes, plump and juicy

and sixty blueberries, small and round. **60**

70 Josephine picked seventy strawberries, sweet and red.

Max picked eighty stringbeans, thin and crisp. **80**

90 Josephine dug ninety potatoes, nobby and brown.

And they picked one hundred ears of corn. **100**

It was not ordinary corn. Max and Josephine saved it for cold winter nights, when the garden was covered with snow. Then they turned it into hundreds and thousands of big white crunchy puffs because that corn was POPCORN!